REFLECTIONS
FOR
LENT 2018

REFLECTIONS
FOR
LENT

14 February – 31 March 2018

GILLIAN COOPER
MARTYN PERCY
JANE WILLIAMS
JEREMY WORTHEN

with an introduction by
CHRISTOPHER HERBERT

Church House Publishing
Church House
Great Smith Street
London SW1P 3AZ

ISBN 978 1 78140 027 2

Published 2017 by Church House Publishing
Copyright © The Archbishops' Council 2017

Liturgical editor: Peter Moger
Series editor: Hugh Hillyard-Parker
Designed and typeset by Hugh Hillyard-Parker
Copy edited by: Ros Connelly
Printed by CPI Group (UK) Ltd, Croydon CR0 4YY

What do you think of *Reflections for Daily Prayer*?

We'd love to hear from you – simply email us at

publishing@churchofengland.org

or write to us at

Church House Publishing, Church House,
Great Smith Street, London SW1P 3AZ.

Visit **www.dailyprayer.org.uk** for more
information on the *Reflections* series, ordering
and subscriptions.

Contents

About the authors

Gillian Cooper is a writer who has previously worked as a theological educator, a cathedral verger, and an administrator. After many years of helping Christians read the Bible, she remains committed to exploring how the Old Testament speaks to life and faith.

Stephen Cottrell is the Bishop of Chelmsford. He is a well-known writer and speaker on evangelism, spirituality and catechesis. He is one of the team that produced *Pilgrim*, the popular course for the Christian Journey.

Christopher Herbert was ordained in Hereford in 1967, becoming a curate and then Diocesan Director of Education. He was an incumbent in Surrey and later, Archdeacon of Dorking. Appointed Bishop of St Albans, he retired in 2009.

Martyn Percy is the Dean of Christ Church, Oxford, one of the University of Oxford's largest colleges, as well as the Cathedral Church of the Diocese of Oxford. From 2004 to 2014 he was Principal of Ripon College, Cuddesdon. Prior to that he was Director of the Lincoln Theological Institute and has also been Chaplain and Director of Studies at Christ's College, Cambridge.

Rachel Treweek is the Bishop of Gloucester and the first female diocesan bishop in England. She served in two parishes in London and was Archdeacon of Northolt and later Hackney. Prior to ordination she was a speech and language therapist and is a trained practitioner in conflict transformation.

Jane Williams is Assistant Dean and Tutor in Theology at St Mellitus College and is a Visiting Lecturer at King's College London. She is the author of a number of books, her most recent being *Why Did Jesus Have to Die?* (2016).

Jeremy Worthen is a priest in the Church of England and is currently the Secretary for Ecumenical Relations and Theology at the Council for Christian Unity. He previously worked in theological education and has written on a range of subjects, including Jewish–Christian relations. His publications include *Responding to God's Call* (2012).

About *Reflections for Lent*

Based on the *Common Worship Lectionary* readings for Morning Prayer, these daily reflections are designed to refresh and inspire times of personal prayer. The aim is to provide rich, contemporary and engaging insights into Scripture.

Each page lists the lectionary readings for the day, with the main psalms for that day highlighted in **bold**. The Collect of the day – either the *Common Worship* collect or the shorter additional collect – is also included.

For those using this book in conjunction with a service of Morning Prayer, the following conventions apply: a psalm printed in parentheses is omitted if it has been used as the opening canticle at that office; a psalm marked with an asterisk may be shortened if desired.

A short reflection is provided on either the Old or New Testament reading. Popular writers, experienced ministers, biblical scholars and theologians contribute to this series, all bringing their own emphases, enthusiasms and approaches to biblical interpretation to bear.

Regular users of Morning Prayer and *Time to Pray* (from *Common Worship: Daily Prayer*) and anyone who follows the lectionary for their regular Bible reading will benefit from the rich variety of traditions represented in these stimulating and accessible pieces.

The book also includes both a simple form of Common Worship: Morning Prayer (see pages 48–49) and a short form of Night Prayer, also known as Compline (see pages 52–55), particularly for the benefit of those readers who are new to the habit of the Daily Office or for any reader while travelling.

Lent – a season of hope and promise

The origins of words are endlessly fascinating. At least, they are for me.

It would seem that our English word 'Lent' derives from the Anglo-Saxon word *'lencten'* which means 'Spring-time'. I like that. It conjures up images of buds bursting like small green spears from twiggy trees; of daffodils pushing up through the ground piercing the air with their delicate, nodding, look-at-me beauty; it hints at lengthening days and warmer sunshine; it evokes the delicious smell of the first cut of new-mown grass. 'Lent' is a glorious word, filled with promise and hope.

Promise and hope, however, are not sentiments that radiate from the predictable and dispiriting sermons and parish magazine articles that so often begin with the disheartening opening phrase: 'Dear Friends, Lent is with us once again ...' The effect can be to deaden the heart. Why? Because one strongly suspects that the message will be that Lent is all about taking on something extra, signing up to group meetings, even more introspection and subtle breast-beating, and probably encouragement to give up something pleasurable.

Of course, careful and honest self-appraisal is never wasted. And, of course, confession, penitence and awareness of our own sinful predilections are to be taken seriously. But if the word 'Lent' refers to Springtime, might that not contain a suggestion that we should also use the time to reflect on the mysteries of new life, of the endless prodigality of the Creation, of the sheer joy of new beginnings, of the presence always of hope, and especially of the utter and inexpressible glory of the Resurrection?

The Reflections that follow in this book will be about all of these things. They will be marked by honesty, by doubt, by faith and by hope. They will have been created out of that demanding exercise best described as 'reflective practice' in which the authors, each with their own unique insights, will have wrestled with biblical texts. But even in that struggle, joy – and, dare I say it – Spring-time are to be found. Spring-time is the new life with which God in his grace refreshes our souls. It is the time and the place where heaven itself steals quietly into our souls helping to re-make us.

And that requires of us patience and a kind of willing-to-be-surprised attention, in which self is forgotten and the renewing beauties of the Creation and the throat-catching challenges of God's Word can make themselves deeply at home in our hearts and in our communities.

One of the truths about Lent is that it exists to give us the assurance that God does indeed make all things new, and whilst Spring-time is not quite with us yet in all its fullness, it is most certainly on its way.

As we are reminded by Canon J.M.C. Crum's lovely Easter hymn, *Now the Green Blade Riseth*, during Lent we prepare ourselves and wait with hope for love to come again, 'like wheat that springeth green'.

Promise, fulfilment and glory are profoundly intertwined.

+Christopher Herbert

Building daily prayer into daily life

In our morning routines there are many tasks we do without giving much thought to them, and others that we do with careful attention. Daily prayer and Bible reading is a strange mixture of these. These are disciplines (and gifts) that we as Christians should have in our daily pattern, but they are not tasks to be ticked off. Rather they are a key component of our developing relationship with God. In them is *life* – for the fruits of this time are to be lived out by us – and to be most fruitful, the task requires both purpose and letting go.

In saying a daily office of prayer, we make the deliberate decision to say 'yes' to spending time with God – the God who is always with us. In prayer and attentive reading of the Scriptures, there is both a conscious entering into God's presence and a 'letting go' of all we strive to control: both are our acknowledgement that it is God who is God.

> *... come before his presence with a song...*
>
> *Know that the Lord is God;*
> *it is he that has made us and we are his;*
> *we are his people and the sheep of his pasture.*
>
> *Enter his gates with thanksgiving...*
>
> *(Psalm 100, a traditional Canticle at Morning Prayer)*

If we want a relationship with someone to deepen and grow, we need to spend time with that person. It can be no surprise that the same is true between us and God.

In our daily routines, I suspect that most of us intentionally look in the mirror; occasionally we might see beyond the surface of our external reflection and catch a glimpse of who we truly are. For me, a regular pattern of daily prayer and Bible reading is like a hard look in a clean mirror: it gives a clear reflection of myself, my life and the world in which I live. But it is more than that, for in it I can also see the reflection of God who is most clearly revealed in Jesus Christ and present with us now in the Holy Spirit.

This commitment to daily prayer is about our relationship with the God who is love. St Paul, in his great passage about love, speaks of now seeing 'in a mirror, dimly' but one day seeing face to face: 'Now I know only in part; then I will know fully, even as I have been fully known' (1 Corinthians 13.12). Our daily prayer is part of that seeing in a mirror dimly, and it is also part of our deep yearning for an ever-clearer vision of our God. As we read Scripture, the past and the future converge in the present moment. We hear words from long ago – some of which can appear strange and confusing – and yet, the Holy Spirit is living and active in the present. In this place of relationship and revelation, we open ourselves to the possibility of being changed, of being reshaped in a way that is good for us and all creation.

It is important that the words of prayer and scripture should penetrate deep within rather than be a mere veneer. A quiet location is therefore a helpful starting point. For some, domestic circumstances or daily schedule make that difficult, but it is never impossible to become more fully present to God. The depths of our being can still be accessed no matter the world's clamour and activity. An awareness of this is all part of our journey from a false sense of control to a place of letting go, to a place where there is an opportunity for transformation.

Sometimes in our attention to Scripture there will be connection with places of joy or pain; we might be encouraged or provoked or both. As we look and see and encounter God more deeply, there will be thanksgiving and repentance; the cries of our heart will surface as we acknowledge our needs and desires for ourselves and the world. The liturgy of Morning Prayer gives this voice and space.

I find it helpful to begin Morning Prayer by lighting a candle. This marks my sense of purpose and my acknowledgement of Christ's presence with me. It is also a silent prayer for illumination as I prepare to be attentive to what I see in the mirror, both of myself and of God. Amid the revelation of Scripture and the cries of my heart, the constancy of the tiny flame bears witness to the hope and light of Christ in all that is and will be.

When the candle is extinguished, I try to be still as I watch the smoke disappear. For me, it is symbolic of my prayers merging with the day. I know that my prayer and the reading of Scripture are not the smoke and mirrors of delusion. Rather, they are about encounter and discovery as I seek to venture into the day to love and serve the Lord as a disciple of Jesus Christ.

+ Rachel Treweek

Lectio Divina – a way of reading the Bible

Lectio Divina is a contemplative way of reading the Bible. It dates back to the early centuries of the Christian Church and was established as a monastic practice by Benedict in the sixth century. It is a way of praying the Scriptures that leads us deeper into God's word. We slow down. We read a short passage more than once. We chew it over slowly and carefully. We savour it. Scripture begins to speak to us in a new way. It speaks to us personally, and aids that union we have with God through Christ, who is himself the Living Word.

Make sure you are sitting comfortably. Breathe slowly and deeply. Ask God to speak to you through the passage that you are about to read.

This way of praying starts with our silence. We often make the mistake of thinking prayer is about what we say to God. It is actually the other way round. God wants to speak to us. He will do this through the Scriptures. So don't worry about what to say. Don't worry if nothing jumps out at you at first. God is patient. He will wait for the opportunity to get in. He will give you a word and lead you to understand its meaning for you today.

First reading: Listen

As you read the passage listen for a word or phrase that attracts you. Allow it to arise from the passage as if it is God's word for you today. Sit in silence repeating the word or phrase in your head.

Then say the word or phrase aloud.

Second reading: Ponder

As you read the passage again, ask how this word or phrase speaks to your life and why it has connected with you. Ponder it carefully. Don't worry if you get distracted – it may be part of your response to offer to God. Sit in silence and then frame a single sentence that begins to say aloud what this word or phrase says to you.

Third reading: Pray

As you read the passage for the last time, ask what Christ is calling from you. What is it that you need to do or consider or relinquish or take on as a result of what God is saying to you in this word or phrase? In the silence that follows the reading, pray for the grace of the Spirit to plant this word in your heart.

If you are in a group, talk for a few minutes and pray with each other.

If you are on your own, speak your prayer to God either aloud or in the silence of your heart.

If there is time, you may even want to read the passage a fourth time, and then end with the same silence before God with which you began.

+Stephen Cottrell

Wednesday 14 February

Ash Wednesday

Psalm **38**
Daniel 9.3-6, 17-19
I Timothy 6.6-19

Daniel 9.3-6, 17-19

*'Lord, great and awesome God,
keeping covenant and steadfast love' (v.4)*

This is both a high point and a low point in the book of Daniel, as it is in the Christian year. Daniel, according to the narrative, has been surprisingly successful. Admittedly, he is in exile, but he has found favour with the king, been allowed to be faithful to his religion, and has been given divine guidance in interpreting dreams.

But now Daniel has hit something he cannot understand. He had been waiting, faithfully, for God to end the exile, as the prophet Jeremiah had foretold, but nothing is happening. Daniel has reached the end of what human intelligence, even with the gift of angelic interpretation, can cope with.

If that is the low point, the high point is Daniel's response: he abandons attempts to read the signs of the times and casts himself on what he knows of God, the God who keeps covenant with faithful love (v.4). Daniel repents, not for his own faults, but for the world that is no longer transparent to God, where we can no longer read the purposes of God, not because God has changed, but because we have lost our way.

Daniel's great insight is that our best hope is that God is always God. Whether we understand what is happening or not, we know that God is faithful and loving. We are dust, but God has breathed life into us.

COLLECT

Almighty and everlasting God,
you hate nothing that you have made
and forgive the sins of all those who are penitent:
create and make in us new and contrite hearts
that we, worthily lamenting our sins
and acknowledging our wretchedness,
may receive from you, the God of all mercy,
perfect remission and forgiveness;
through Jesus Christ your Son our Lord,
who is alive and reigns with you,
in the unity of the Holy Spirit,
one God, now and for ever.

Reflection by **Jane Williams**

Psalm **77** *or* **37***
Genesis 39
Galatians 2.11-end

Thursday 15 February

Genesis 39

'The Lord was with him' (v.23)

This is the first time we encounter the Lord in the story of Joseph. Whereas with Abraham, Isaac and Jacob, God appeared and spoke to them, with Joseph, God works behind the scenes and we need the narrator's help to read the divine actions. God enables Joseph to prosper at work, for example, but does not protect him from the advances of Potiphar's wife: there are bigger things at stake here than just Joseph's well-being.

Without his father's fond protection, Joseph is growing up fast. There was no indication, when he lived at home and teased his brothers, that he had a gift for leadership and management, but alone, enslaved, he proves a successful steward. Unlike Jacob, God is not cossetting Joseph but training him for the next step. The old Joseph is not entirely gone: the boy who boasted that he was more important than all his brothers – and even his father – now boasts that he is as great as his master. Joseph still stirs up strong emotions wherever he goes, and Potiphar and his wife react with passion, with anger, with jealousy – all emotions Joseph has provoked before. Only the Lord does not over-react to Joseph, acting only in response to his own nature, not Joseph's. The Lord shows Joseph the steadfast love he has never known before, and so Joseph continues to grow towards his destiny.

Holy God,
our lives are laid open before you:
rescue us from the chaos of sin
and through the death of your Son
bring us healing and make us whole
in Jesus Christ our Lord.

COLLECT

Reflection by **Jane Williams**   9

Friday 16 February

Genesis 40

'Do not interpretations belong to God?' (v.8)

There is a glimpse today of the arbitrary world that slaves inhabit. Joseph is in prison because of the lies and jealousy of his employers, and is joined by Pharaoh's baker and cupbearer, who are equally here at the whim of someone more powerful than themselves. But there is hierarchy even among imprisoned slaves, and so Joseph, no longer anyone's spoilt darling, is a servant to the servants of Pharaoh. They treat him as they have been treated: they use him when it suits them, and forget him when it doesn't; they have little interest in his story of abduction and wrongful arrest, and when the cupbearer is duly restored to his place of favour, as Joseph predicted, he forgets him instantly.

What hard lessons Joseph is learning about himself and his value in the world. They are lessons that will stand him in good stead when he finally comes to power, and they will enable him to value his family properly when he meets them again, but alone, forgotten, in prison, Joseph does not know this.

We are not told if Joseph feels God's presence. Certainly, for the first time, Joseph acknowledges God's role in dreams and their interpretation – something he didn't mention when crowing over his brothers. From the safety of narrative omniscience, we know that God is with him, and perhaps we can be comforted, too, by the knowledge that a hidden God is not an absent one.

COLLECT

Almighty and everlasting God,
you hate nothing that you have made
and forgive the sins of all those who are penitent:
create and make in us new and contrite hearts
that we, worthily lamenting our sins
and acknowledging our wretchedness,
may receive from you, the God of all mercy,
perfect remission and forgiveness;
through Jesus Christ your Son our Lord,
who is alive and reigns with you,
in the unity of the Holy Spirit,
one God, now and for ever.

Reflection by **Jane Williams**

Psalm 71 *or* 41, **42, 43**
Genesis 41.1-24
Galatians 3.15-22

Saturday 17 February

Genesis 41.1-24

'It is not I; God will give Pharaoh a favourable answer' (v.16)

There is a kind of gentle humour at work in this story. Joseph's interest in dreams is what got him into trouble in the first place, and now God is going to use that interest to get him out of it again. But the humour also points up a theological assumption: human action and God's action work in different ways and are not in competition. Joseph could tell his story, at this point, as one of hardship, of being abandoned by his family and his God: he has now been in prison, apparently forgotten, for two years. That perspective would not be untruthful, in terms of the human actions so far, but it leaves out God's actions. Even though God does not speak directly to Joseph, that does not mean that God has left himself without ways to communicate.

Most cultures are fascinated by dreams and the powerful sense of profound but hidden meaning they carry. As a king, Pharaoh would expect his dreams to be of great significance – an obvious channel from the divine realm to the divine ruler on earth. His dreams in this case are fairly self-explanatory, so much so, that his own interpreters must either have been useless or too scared to explain what was coming. But Joseph seizes the chance that God has given him, with all the confidence of a favourite son, confidence still somewhere in him, after all this time.

Holy God,
our lives are laid open before you:
rescue us from the chaos of sin
and through the death of your Son
bring us healing and make us whole
in Jesus Christ our Lord.

COLLECT

Reflection by **Jane Williams**

Monday 19 February

Psalms 10, 11 *or* 44
Genesis 41.25-45
Galatians 3.23 – 4.7

Genesis 41.25-45

*'Since God has shown you all this,
there is no one so discerning and wise as you' (v.39)*

Pharaoh's dream is terrible and clear. Egypt's economy is based on cattle and agriculture, fed by the fertile waters of the Nile. The thin cows and the empty ears of grain are a nightmarish foretaste of what is to come. We hear the dream three times in this chapter: twice from Pharaoh and once as Joseph interprets it, so there can be no mistake about its grim portent, or its divine origin. No wonder Pharaoh's own interpreters did not want to tell him what it meant.

But Joseph is not a professional court interpreter, and he feels no need to stop at explaining what the dream means. Just hauled out of prison, clean, properly dressed and shaved for the first time in two years, Joseph has the courage to tell Pharaoh what to do. The narrator lets Pharaoh show us how this is possible: it is Pharaoh who points out that Joseph speaks with the authority of God (vv.38-39).

Instantly, Joseph's world is different. Instantly, he becomes Pharaoh's representative in the land, with people bowing before him, a new name, a new wife, a new world. The spare narration of this story does not tell us how Joseph the interpreter read his own circumstances, whether he thought this was God acting on his behalf, of whether he knew that he was part of something bigger. Not that those two are mutually exclusive, of course.

COLLECT

Almighty God,
whose Son Jesus Christ fasted forty days in the wilderness,
and was tempted as we are, yet without sin:
give us grace to discipline ourselves in obedience to your Spirit;
and, as you know our weakness,
so may we know your power to save;
through Jesus Christ your Son our Lord,
who is alive and reigns with you,
in the unity of the Holy Spirit,
one God, now and for ever.

| *Reflection by* **Jane Williams**

Psalm **44** *or* **48**, 52
Genesis 41.46 – 42.5
Galatians 4.8-20

Genesis 41.46 – 42.5

*'God has made me forget all my hardship
and all my father's house' (v.51)*

Pharaoh and Joseph are showing extraordinary confidence in God. Joseph is given absolute authority to go through all the cities of Egypt and commandeer grain and food and put it away in storage. For seven whole years of plentiful harvests, this foreigner is given permission to take away the fruits of the labour of the local farmers who must, surely, have been sceptical about the so-called famine that was meant to be coming. There must have been muttering and anger against Joseph, suspicions that he was just lining his own pockets. But Joseph and Pharaoh have shared that moment of certainty about God's presence and meaning, and neither questions at all.

While Joseph is unswervingly obeying God and his new master, Pharaoh, he is also trying to convince himself that he is happy and settled, free of the past. But the names he gives his children suggest otherwise: they are family names, not Egyptian ones, and the very fact that they speak of forgetting and contentment suggests that Joseph does not yet have either.

And now the past that he thinks he has dismissed is about to return, as the famine begins to bite beyond the borders of Egypt and the narrative swings back from Joseph's changed life to the unchanged tension between Jacob and his remaining sons. Jacob is still nagging his older sons and still favouring his younger son. Time, that has transformed Joseph, has done little for Jacob.

Heavenly Father,
your Son battled with the powers of darkness,
and grew closer to you in the desert:
help us to use these days to grow in wisdom and prayer
that we may witness to your saving love
in Jesus Christ our Lord.

COLLECT

Reflection by **Jane Williams** | 13

Wednesday 21 February

Psalms **6**, 17 *or* **119.57-80**
Genesis 42.6-17
Galatians 4.21 – 5.1

Genesis 42.6-17

'Joseph's brothers came and bowed themselves before him with their faces to the ground' (v.6)

The author of the Joseph story has already trained us to see what is going on from more than one perspective: how it might be viewed if we didn't know God was at work, and how we view it, knowing that God is. Now this layering technique is going to switch back and forth, from Joseph to his brothers and then back to us, as we see with the narrator's knowledge.

So we, and Joseph, see the irony as Joseph's brothers come back on the scene, bowing to him, calling themselves his servants, thinking that they are describing only themselves as 'sons of one man', little realizing that they are also describing the great official in front of them. We and Joseph remember Joseph's dream, and see it fulfilled, though the brothers do not. We and Joseph understand why Joseph does not immediately reveal himself to the brothers who sold him into slavery. We and Joseph see that three days in prison is not a lot, compared with the years that Joseph spent there. And we understand why Joseph needs to find out whether fraternal love and loyalty have grown in his absence.

We, with the narrator, see how much Joseph has changed, from the brat who would certainly have used his new position to boast to his brothers, to the statesman, but also to the man who longs to know if anything can be saved from his own bitter past.

COLLECT

Almighty God,
whose Son Jesus Christ fasted forty days in the wilderness,
and was tempted as we are, yet without sin:
give us grace to discipline ourselves in obedience to your Spirit;
and, as you know our weakness,
so may we know your power to save;
through Jesus Christ your Son our Lord,
who is alive and reigns with you,
in the unity of the Holy Spirit,
one God, now and for ever.

14 | *Reflection by* **Jane Williams**

Psalms **42**, 43 *or* 56, **57** (63*)
Genesis 42.18-28
Galatians 5.2-15

Thursday 22 February

Genesis 42.18-28

'He turned away from them and wept' (v.24)

While we, the readers, have been following Joseph's story, his brothers have been left behind, dealing with the consequences of their actions. Now we get a glimpse into the tortured years the brothers have suffered. Their guilt has bitten deep: it is as though they have been waiting, ever since, for this moment when they will have to pay. Reuben's anguished, 'I told you so!' gets no response because it has been said so often between the brothers. They are wholly turned in on their shared burden, utterly unaware that the foreign official can understand them.

Very briefly, the focus shifts back to Joseph, weeping. This is what he has longed to hear: that he is not forgotten, that he is regretted, that his brothers have not just carried on, happy and unconcerned. Joseph's power, grandeur, new wife, new children are not enough to make him a new identity; for that, he needs his brothers' love.

It's hard to tell whether it is a desire for revenge or a residual insecurity that prolongs the anguish, postpones the moment when Joseph reveals himself. But the test he sets his brothers suggests the latter: will they abandon Simeon, now that they have what they came for? Will they treat him as they treated Joseph, as expendable? Or have they learned loyalty the hard way?

Heavenly Father,
your Son battled with the powers of darkness,
and grew closer to you in the desert:
help us to use these days to grow in wisdom and prayer
that we may witness to your saving love
in Jesus Christ our Lord.

COLLECT

Reflection by **Jane Williams**   15

Friday 23 February

Psalm **22** *or* **51**, 54
Genesis 42.29-end
Galatians 5.16-end

Genesis 42.29-end

*'I am the one you have bereaved of children ...
All this has happened to me!' (v.36)*

In this final section of chapter 42, we see the world that Joseph's brothers have been living in. Jacob is one of the least lovable characters in stories of the patriarchs, with his underhanded plot to get his brother's birth right. The trickster is tricked in his turn, marries the wrong wife and has to wait for the right one, and that legacy of duplicity and favouritism is what we see played out in this narrative of Joseph. Jacob is also, of course, a mystic and seer, one who encounters God in vivid and intimate ways. But it is surely no accident that Jacob the cheat is left with a permanent limp when he wrestles with the angel.

The brothers may have been changed by remorse, but it seems that Jacob has not. He may or may not have his suspicions about how Joseph disappeared, but it is clear that he has made his sons pay every day for the fact that they are not Joseph. He is still making Leah's children feel that they are not truly his, as though the fault of their birth is theirs. It is terrible to hear how Reuben has absorbed that message, so that he is willing to offer his own children as surety against Benjamin's safety.

There is no hint from the narrator here that this is God at work. God will deal with what happens, but our choices are real, as are those of Jacob and his sons.

COLLECT

Almighty God,
whose Son Jesus Christ fasted forty days in the wilderness,
and was tempted as we are, yet without sin:
give us grace to discipline ourselves in obedience to your Spirit;
and, as you know our weakness,
so may we know your power to save;
through Jesus Christ your Son our Lord,
who is alive and reigns with you,
in the unity of the Holy Spirit,
one God, now and for ever.

| *Reflection by* **Jane Williams**

Psalms 59, **63** *or* **68**
Genesis 43.1-15
Galatians 6

Saturday 24 February

Genesis 43.1-15

'Why did you treat me so badly as to tell the man that you had another brother?' (v.6)

Hunger finally drives Jacob to give in. He has been willing to manage without Simeon, left imprisoned in Egypt, rather than risk Benjamin, but now crisis has come: Benjamin or Jacob? Inevitably, Jacob chooses himself. This time, it is Judah, not Reuben, who bargains with Jacob, but there is a kind of hypocrisy about the bargain. Reuben had offered his own sons if he failed to bring Benjamin safely home, but Judah just says, trust me, and stop fussing. Judah, it seems, is the practical one. It was his idea to sell Joseph into slavery, rather than leaving him in the pit to die, whereas Reuben had been planning to save Joseph behind his brothers' back.

Jacob gives in, with as much bad grace as he can. 'Bring back your other brother (whose name I can't be bothered with) and Benjamin', he says.

Leah's children always seem to have to act as a single entity in Jacob's eyes. They may have wives and children of their own, but for Jacob, they are the expendable sons, whose job it is to work for him and to look after Joseph and Benjamin, Rachel's children. The subsequent history of Israel suggests that that is not how God sees them: God chooses the twelve tribes, and Jesus chooses twelve to help him reconstitute the kingdom of love.

Heavenly Father,
your Son battled with the powers of darkness,
and grew closer to you in the desert:
help us to use these days to grow in wisdom and prayer
that we may witness to your saving love
in Jesus Christ our Lord.

COLLECT

Monday 26 February

Genesis 43.16-end

'So they drank and were merry with him' (v.34)

It was a very different affair, the last time the brothers ate when Joseph was with them. They weren't in a house in Egypt with various attendants, but alone in the fields at Dothan. Joseph wasn't sitting with them then either, but that's because they had thrown him in a pit, without even water (Genesis 37.16-25). Now they are enjoying the portions he sends down from his table. Then the big topic of conversation was how to get rid of him; we're not told what they're talking about here, but they seem to be having a good time. Joseph's lavish hospitality has dulled the jumpiness and bad conscience that have marked their expedition so far.

A meal is an occasion to celebrate the goodness of God in creation, and the particular blessing of human relationships. Yet it can also show up the shadows of sin and of human tragedy. At the meals we will be part of this week, will there be people, like Joseph, with a secret that could change everything, but which they fear – perhaps with good reason – to declare? Will there be people, like the brothers in Egypt, trying to block out feelings of guilt and shame by throwing themselves into the party? Will there even be people like the brothers in Dothan, heedless of suffering they are inflicting on others, wishing them out of sight and mind? And will any of those people be us?

COLLECT

Almighty God,
you show to those who are in error the light of your truth,
that they may return to the way of righteousness:
grant to all those who are admitted
    into the fellowship of Christ's religion,
that they may reject those things
    that are contrary to their profession,
and follow all such things as are agreeable to the same;
through our Lord Jesus Christ,
who is alive and reigns with you,
in the unity of the Holy Spirit,
one God, now and for ever.

Reflection by **Jeremy Worthen**

Psalm **50** *or* **73**
Genesis 44.1-17
Hebrews 2.1-9

Tuesday 27 February

Genesis 44.1-17

'Joseph said to his steward, "Go, follow after the men"' (v.4)

It is taking a while, this story about the brothers meeting Joseph in Egypt. Old Testament narrative can sketch out the most profound events in a few elliptical sentences, but here we have detail on detail as the plot twists this way and that.

It is taking a while, because Joseph is taking his time. He knows who they are the moment he sees them – and what they did to him. He also knows how deeply he longs to be with Benjamin, his brother, with Jacob, his father, and with his whole family, together. But this is not something that can be quickly resolved.

Joseph is taking his time, because reconciliation takes time. Whenever it happens, it is a kind of miracle, an event of grace, but also a long and difficult journey, the slow work of healing and restoration of trust. The fear is always that the script will just run again: those who harmed, those who abused, will harm and abuse again as soon as the circumstances are right. So Joseph sets a test. Once more, the favourite son, the youngest son, is away from the protection of his father. The other brothers can walk out of trouble and back into freedom if they would only dump Benjamin, make up a lie and forget him too.

Reconciliation takes time. Those who are called to the ministry of reconciliation must therefore be willing to wait, with prayer and compassion, for the journey to unfold and the miracle to come.

Almighty God,
by the prayer and discipline of Lent
may we enter into the mystery of Christ's sufferings,
and by following in his Way
come to share in his glory;
through Jesus Christ our Lord.

COLLECT

Reflection by **Jeremy Worthen** | 19

Wednesday 28 February

Genesis 44.18-end

'... a slave to my lord in place of the boy' (v.33)

Judah has changed. In chapter 42, Reuben, the eldest, spoke for the brothers, but it was Judah who persuaded Jacob to let them return to Egypt with Benjamin, and it is Judah who, at this critical juncture of the story, turns its shifting direction decisively towards reconciliation.

Judah has changed. The one who persuaded the others to sell their youngest brother into slavery (Genesis 37.26-27) offers to become a slave himself so that the youngest can go free. Yet this is not a case of conversion to philosophical altruism. What comes across most strongly in Judah's speech – the longest speech in the book of Genesis – is his love for his father, his willingness to lay down his own life for the sake of the happiness of his father's final days. Did he not love his father before? Yes, in a way, but a way that made him so resentful of the love Jacob had for Joseph that he wanted to make sure that the father would lose the beloved son forever. Now again, 'his life is bound up in the boy's life', but there is no resentment, no jealousy, no hatred. Instead, his love for his father means he will protect at any cost the brother his father loves.

May our hearts be so full of love for God that our only care is the salvation of that which God loves, God's life bound up in it, the world for which the Father gave the only-begotten Son.

Reflection by **Jeremy Worthen**

Psalm **34** *or* **78.1-39***
Genesis 45.1-15
Hebrews 3.1-6

Thursday 1 March

Genesis 45.1-15

'God sent me before you to preserve life' (v.5)

The tension that has been building finally breaks. Joseph reveals himself to his brothers, accepting that this means undergoing a loss of control, as he lets the grief that had been frozen in his heart and the joy for which he had not dared to hope course through him and overwhelm him.

Surely there would have been so very many things he wanted to say to them. But there is really only one thing he tells them in this first, momentous encounter: God sent me here. He knows they are frightened, bewildered, confused, so he wisely tells them not once but three times, in verses 5–8: God sent me here. And the word for 'send' he uses is the same one that resonates through the many stories of vocation in the Old Testament and that stands behind those that follow from them in the New.

Joseph is not naïve about what happened, and the man running the imperial economy can hardly be characterized as otherworldly. He sees the complexities of human agency, yet beneath and above it all he discerns God's agency. He sees the sin mixed up with human action, which flared up in his brothers' wicked deed, but he perceives that God is always working for life (the Hebrew word for which appears in verses 5 and 7), faithful to the promise. And he knows that he has a part in that promise: he has been called, he has been sent. The strong root of his wisdom.

Almighty God,
by the prayer and discipline of Lent
may we enter into the mystery of Christ's sufferings,
and by following in his Way
come to share in his glory;
through Jesus Christ our Lord.

COLLECT

Reflection by **Jeremy Worthen**   21

Friday 2 March

Genesis 45.16-end

'... the spirit of their father Jacob revived' (v.27)

The Hebrew term for 'revived' used here is the same word that was key to the first part of the chapter: the verb whose basic meaning is 'to live'. Jacob's spirit 'lives' or 'comes alive' as he comes to believe the unbelievable good news that Joseph is still living. As the switching between the names 'Jacob' and 'Israel' in this section reminds us, the one person represents the people, and the people cannot live incomplete, the life of the whole without the life of all.

Not every story of fraternal jealousy, or human trafficking, or false accusation, ends as happily as the story of Joseph, of course. Sometimes there is no reconciliation or end to grief. Sometimes people die of violence or neglect. Sometimes those who do wicked deeds live on in prosperity and apparent peace, indifferent to what they have done.

Luke says of the disciples meeting the risen Jesus that at first 'in their joy they were disbelieving' (Luke 24.41). Like Jacob, they cannot believe that what they thought was lost has been restored and transformed in a way they could never have imagined. The good news of Christ is that death does not triumph, and that no loss, no failure, no evil and no tragedy can deal death to the spirit of those who are alive in Christ Jesus. In him, we are called to share in the story of Israel, as people of hope, people who do not give up.

COLLECT

Almighty God,
you show to those who are in error the light of your truth,
that they may return to the way of righteousness:
grant to all those who are admitted
    into the fellowship of Christ's religion,
that they may reject those things
    that are contrary to their profession,
and follow all such things as are agreeable to the same;
through our Lord Jesus Christ,
who is alive and reigns with you,
in the unity of the Holy Spirit,
one God, now and for ever.

Reflection by **Jeremy Worthen**

Psalms 3, **25** *or* **76**, 79
Genesis 46.1-7, 28-end
Hebrews 4.1-13

Saturday 3 March

Genesis 46.1-7, 28-end

'I myself will go down with you' (v.4)

The case for emigration is very clear: starvation in Canaan, with no one to help, versus a stable supply of food in Egypt, administered by Jacob's beloved son, sent there by God to provide for them all. Yet all the same, Jacob hesitates. He is leaving the land of God's promise to enter alien territory. Can this really be part of the plan?

This is the only time in the Joseph story that God speaks directly, with a promise of presence and of restoration. Verse 4 twice uses the emphatic pronoun for 'I' in Hebrew where it is not required grammatically: 'I myself will go down with you to Egypt, and I [myself] will also bring you up again.' This is, at it were, a detour, to a place that is not and cannot be home: but God will be there. At the same time, the God who goes with him and whose presence he will not lose is also the one who will restore the body of Jacob and the life of Israel to their true, abiding home.

Not every place to which God calls us to go is somewhere we should stay, or put down deep roots of attachment. We can be confident that if God calls us, then God goes with us, and however strange and hard the road may be, we will not lose God's presence. But we also need to remember where home is, the place prepared for us, the promise that awaits us.

Almighty God,
by the prayer and discipline of Lent
may we enter into the mystery of Christ's sufferings,
and by following in his Way
come to share in his glory;
through Jesus Christ our Lord.

COLLECT

Reflection by **Jeremy Worthen** | 23

Monday 5 March

Genesis 47.1-27

'Jacob blessed Pharaoh' (v.7)

Jacob blesses Pharaoh; Israel blesses Egypt – not once but twice (vv. 7 and 10). It could be argued that this denotes no more than a formal greeting and then leave taking, yet it seems unlikely that the resonance of the word in this context should be treated entirely casually. Jacob is a frail old man, reliant on his famous son, a suppliant seeking a place to live, indeed the basic means to live, from the most powerful person on earth, so far as he is aware. And Jacob blesses Pharaoh; Israel blesses Egypt – not once but twice.

Jacob also has a word for Pharaoh. The inquiry about his age is no more than formal politeness. For us, to ask someone their age is seen as rudeness, as if length of years were a thing to be ashamed of; here, it is the opposite. Jacob initially responds in conventional fashion, underlining the span of his life with suitable modesty, but then draws attention to the case of his ancestors, whose election was marked with even greater abundance. Yet for them as for him, this is all a 'sojourn' – a dwelling in a land that is not one's final home, whether in Ur or in Canaan or in Egypt. 'They confessed that they were strangers and foreigners on the earth, for people who speak in this way make it clear that they are seeking a homeland' (Hebrews 11.13b–14).

A subtle word, and an unobtrusive blessing; who can say with what effect?

COLLECT

Almighty God,
whose most dear Son went not up to joy but first he suffered pain,
and entered not into glory before he was crucified:
mercifully grant that we, walking in the way of the cross,
may find it none other than the way of life and peace;
through Jesus Christ your Son our Lord,
who is alive and reigns with you,
in the unity of the Holy Spirit,
one God, now and for ever.

Reflection by **Jeremy Worthen**

Psalms 6, **9** *or* 87, **89.1-18**   **Tuesday 6 March**
Genesis 47.28 – 48.end
Hebrews 5.11 – 6.12

Genesis 47.28 – 48.end

'I buried her there on the way to Ephrath' (48.7)

Jacob is ill and dying, but he must pass on his blessing to Joseph and his sons. To do that, he begins by remembering how he was blessed by God, many years previously. That memory causes him to mention two names that have been more or less absent from Genesis since the focus moved to Joseph and his brothers in chapter 37.

The first is Rachel. Though she appears in the genealogical list in chapter 46, and her death in childbirth, recorded in Genesis 35.16–21, colours everything that follows, only now is she spoken of directly. Her death follows immediately after God's appearing to Jacob, so it seems that to recall God's blessing moves him to speak also of his loss.

The second is Abraham. God who blesses Jacob in Genesis 35.9–15 names Abraham along with Isaac, and now Jacob mentions Abraham and Isaac twice in his blessing of Joseph and his sons. To share in the blessing is to stand in the line of Abraham; the story that begins with his call goes on, because the promise of God does not fail.

We want to bring blessing to others. To do that, we need to remember how we have received the blessing of God, for we have no other to pass on. That means that our blessing of others will be marked by what has happened to us, our old scars and open wounds, to draw them also into the one story of God's promise, God's steadfast love.

Eternal God,
give us insight
to discern your will for us,
to give up what harms us,
and to seek the perfection we are promised
in Jesus Christ our Lord.

COLLECT

Reflection by **Jeremy Worthen**   25

Wednesday 7 March

Psalm **38** *or* **119.105-128**
Genesis 49.1-32
Hebrews 6.13-end

Genesis 49.1-32

'I wait for your salvation, O Lord' (v.18)

Jacob's parting words to his sons form the first extended poem in the Bible. Full of Hebrew word play and obscure expressions, it is very difficult to translate. It is also hard to know what we are to make of it. A kind of prophecy? Perhaps. Some of the sayings in this collection seem to refer to events that have already happened to the characters (e.g. vv.4 and 6), others to the future fortunes of the tribes once they have returned to Canaan (e.g. vv.13 and 19). For centuries, Jewish and Christian interpreters saw messianic meaning in verse 10, though disagreeing passionately about what exactly it might be.

Confronted by so many puzzles, we might be tempted to imagine that verse 18 was despairingly inserted by a similarly perplexed ancient scribe, whose standard for sacred poetry was the psalms. But this poem, this prophecy, is an act of faithful waiting. Jacob senses there is a long road ahead, and that it will not be simple or straightforward. His descendants will return to the land of God's promise, but that will not be the end of history but only a further chapter, in which sin, struggle and suffering will still feature heavily. There remains, however, a horizon beyond that, a horizon that looms darkly, obscurely, in the blessing of Joseph in verses 24–26: unbreakable blessing, powerful beyond all the powers of creation, from one who provides for us, saves us and cares for us like a shepherd.

COLLECT

Almighty God,
whose most dear Son went not up to joy but first he suffered pain,
and entered not into glory before he was crucified:
mercifully grant that we, walking in the way of the cross,
may find it none other than the way of life and peace;
through Jesus Christ your Son our Lord,
who is alive and reigns with you,
in the unity of the Holy Spirit,
one God, now and for ever.

Reflection by **Jeremy Worthen**

Psalms **56**, 57 *or* 90, **92**
Genesis 49.33 – 50.end
Hebrews 7.1-10

Thursday 8 March

Genesis 49.33 – 50.end

'... forgive the crime of your brothers' (50.17)

Perhaps only in fiction or at a distance are repentance and forgiveness simple, instantaneous events. Are the brothers truly sorry for what they did to Joseph, or merely afraid of the possible consequences with their father no longer around? Fear leads them once again to lie, as they lied to Jacob for decades about Joseph, yet in their deceit they nonetheless speak a kind of truth. They use the words 'wrong' and 'crime' for the first time in the narrative to refer to what they did, and it is in their own name, and not that of their father, that they finally ask to be forgiven.

If their repentance is not straightforward, neither perhaps is Joseph's forgiveness. He never says to them, 'I forgive you.' Indeed, his rhetorical question to them, 'Am I in the place of God?', might be taken as a refusal to offer a forgiveness only God can grant, as well as to enact a judgement only God can determine. But what Joseph does is refrain from seeking vengeance, and, more than that, he continues to do good to those who had wronged him, both through material provision and through the moral quality of his communication with them. He has come to see what happened in the light of God's unshakeable purpose for good; he will not let their 'crime' – which he acknowledges – define his or their existence.

Without grace drawing repentance and forgiveness together into the deepening mystery of reconciliation, the Bible would have ended here.

Eternal God,
give us insight
to discern your will for us,
to give up what harms us,
and to seek the perfection we are promised
in Jesus Christ our Lord.

COLLECT

Reflection by **Jeremy Worthen** | 27

Friday 9 March

Psalm **22** *or* **88** (95)
Exodus 1.1-14
Hebrews 7.11-end

Exodus 1.1-14

'Come, let us deal shrewdly with them' (v.10)

If fascination can be a compound of fear, attraction and control, then the new Pharaoh and his people are fascinated by the Israelites. They are intimidated by their numbers and their strength, strength that could make them a military threat if their loyalty cannot be guaranteed. Yet the obvious solution to that – that they relocate back to Canaan – appears only as the final stage in Pharaoh's worst-case scenario in verse 10. No, they want to keep them near. And the way to stay close to what is dangerous is to control it, pressure it relentlessly into submission, break its power.

Ultimately, this fascination proves self-destructive. The energy pulsing through the children of Israel cannot be contained by human means, no matter how shrewd or ruthless those means may be. Fascination leads to escalating, damaging conflict, preventing Pharaoh from acceding to the request that would have been liberation for him, as well as for the Hebrews: 'Let my people go' (Exodus 9.1). It only ends with the drowning of his army, his power, in the waters of the Red Sea.

Fascination of this kind is the distortion of desire, to which the only true antidote is love, which casts out fear and seeks the release of the beloved from all that blocks its flourishing. It is perhaps easy to persuade ourselves that fascination with what is good is itself a kind of goodness, when it may turn out to be a creeping paralysis that shuts us off from the path of life.

COLLECT

Almighty God,
whose most dear Son went not up to joy but first he suffered pain,
and entered not into glory before he was crucified:
mercifully grant that we, walking in the way of the cross,
may find it none other than the way of life and peace;
through Jesus Christ your Son our Lord,
who is alive and reigns with you,
in the unity of the Holy Spirit,
one God, now and for ever.

Reflection by **Jeremy Worthen**

Psalm 31 *or* 96, 97, 100
Exodus 1.22 – 2.10
Hebrews 8

Saturday 10 March

Exodus 1.22 – 2.10
'He was crying, and she took pity on him' (2.6)

However high the walls may rise between communities, there are likely to be occasions when encounter still happens, so that common humanity can become the exceptional ground for communication and cracks may even begin to appear across them. The decision of Moses' mother to put him in a papyrus basket has nothing to do with wanting to attract the attention of Egyptians: a pragmatic hiding place away from living quarters, and literalistic (even parodic?) compliance with Pharaoh's chilling command. Yet the basket becomes the place where Egyptian meets Hebrew, suffering evokes pity, pity leads to care, and care brings lasting interchange between the two communities, focused on a single person but with effects that will change them both irrevocably.

Pharaoh's daughter's life would have been carefully designed to ensure she never heard the cries of the oppressed Israelites. But somehow, those cries impinge on her world, and she responds with a simple act of compassion. Moreover, she recognizes immediately that she does not possess by herself, for all her riches, the means to provide the care that is required: help for the Hebrew must involve the Hebrews, without her just walking away and leaving the situation to them.

Are there people around you who are suffering, but whose cries you never hear? Are there cries you are hearing today, and call on your compassion? Might you be called to act and take a share of responsibility, not alone but with others, including those whose cries these are?

Eternal God,
give us insight
to discern your will for us,
to give up what harms us,
and to seek the perfection we are promised
in Jesus Christ our Lord.

COLLECT

Reflection by **Jeremy Worthen**   29

Monday 12 March

Exodus 2.11-22

'... an alien residing in a foreign land' (v.22)

God's big plan is in tatters. The descendants of Abraham, chosen by God to be his own people in a land of their own, are slaves in Egypt. Worse, they are victims of attempted genocide. One baby boy miraculously survives – but through his own stupidity and violence has to run away from his family and home. We need to forget we have read this story before, and recognize a hopeless situation. These people seem capable of destroying themselves if Pharaoh does not do it first.

Yet there are perhaps signs of hope. Moses' fighting skills are put to better use when they help him acquire a new family. He is also learning the hard way what it means to be a Hebrew. We assume he now knows his true identity, but this is the first time he has felt what it is like to be in danger and to live in exile. The boy brought up in a royal palace is being hardened into the man he is destined to be.

The story told by Exodus is one of God's infinite persistence. Even on occasions when God's patience seems to run out, a way is found for the plan to go forward. Promises have been made, and God will not break them, however badly his people behave. It is good news for Israel, and good news for us, unworthy recipients of God's promises that we are.

COLLECT

Merciful Lord,
absolve your people from their offences,
that through your bountiful goodness
we may all be delivered from the chains of those sins
which by our frailty we have committed;
grant this, heavenly Father,
for Jesus Christ's sake, our blessed Lord and Saviour,
who is alive and reigns with you,
in the unity of the Holy Spirit,
one God, now and for ever.

Reflection by **Gillian Cooper**

Psalms 54, **79** *or* **106*** *(or* 103)
Exodus 2.23 – 3.20
Hebrews 9.15-end

Tuesday 13 March

Exodus 2.23 – 3.20

'God remembered his covenant' (2.24)

Who is this God, who remembers his promises? Moses needs to know, he thinks, if he is to be believed. He demands a name. God's answer is enigmatic in the extreme. For all the best efforts of scholars, we do not know what to make of 'I am who I am'. We are not helped by the nature of tenses in Hebrew verbs. Is it 'I will be who I will be'? Or perhaps 'I am who I will be'?

Moses needs to listen more carefully. Three times he is told who this God is: 'the God of Abraham, the God of Isaac, and the God of Jacob'. Other gods have names: lesser gods, members of divine families. The God of Israel needs no name to pin him down. He is defined by something much more dynamic. He has been active in the lives of the ancestors of the Hebrews. He has made promises. He has paid attention to their plight. He has been preparing to act. He has analysed the difficulties. He has chosen and prepared his messenger and given him a message. A land is waiting.

Past, present or future – this God is who he is in every tense. Israel will call him Yahweh, but avoid saying the name by replacing it with 'Lord'. No name, no graven image, nothing fixed, but a living, moving force in the life of Israel and of his people for all time.

Merciful Lord,
you know our struggle to serve you:
when sin spoils our lives
and overshadows our hearts,
come to our aid
and turn us back to you again;
through Jesus Christ our Lord.

COLLECT

Reflection by **Gillian Cooper**   31

Wednesday 14 March

Exodus 4.1-23

'O my Lord, please send someone else' (v.13)

Moses is not as inspired as he should be, and we wonder whether God has made the right choice. Not that we do not feel a certain sympathy alongside our impatience. After all, the task seems suicidal, although we might expect that having seen the burning bush, Moses would have more grasp of God's power to achieve the impossible.

We all know the temptation of making excuses when we know we have to do something hard. In Moses' case, it is the talking he is particularly worried about. This is the first we hear about a brother, but Aaron is literally an answer to prayer. Moses runs out of arguments, and sets off back to Egypt.

Verses 21 to 23 contain a little theological interlude that seems to interrupt the story. We are heading for the account of a marathon battle of wills and magic between God and Moses on one side and Pharaoh on the other. So why is it not all over before it starts? Surely God cannot lose?

The writer explains. It is God who hardens Pharaoh's heart, to make the victory all the more emphatic when it comes. It is a question for us too. If God is omnipotent, how can human beings resist him? We have been given free will, we believe. Our writer however offers us an alternative answer, that God can sometimes create his own difficulties. It is something for us to ponder.

COLLECT

Merciful Lord,
absolve your people from their offences,
that through your bountiful goodness
we may all be delivered from the chains of those sins
which by our frailty we have committed;
grant this, heavenly Father,
for Jesus Christ's sake, our blessed Lord and Saviour,
who is alive and reigns with you,
in the unity of the Holy Spirit,
one God, now and for ever.

Reflection by **Gillian Cooper**

Exodus 4.27 – 6.1

'... you have done nothing at all' (5.23)

The first part is easy. Moses and Aaron follow instructions and are recognized by the Israelites as messengers from the God of their ancestors. They will soon discover the fickleness of public opinion.

The battle begins. Moses and Aaron invent a threat in order to persuade Pharaoh that the people are only going into the desert for a religious observance. Pharaoh, however, is not fooled, and he has no intention of losing his workforce. His answer, like that of many tyrants after him, is to ensure that his slaves are even more firmly under his thumb by making impossible demands and ruthlessly punishing their failure. Predictably, the people's leaders turn on Moses and Aaron, who have made matters much worse with their stupid demand. Equally predictably, Moses then turns on the Lord. The journey to freedom has not begun well. The main characters in the drama are behaving in a typically human way. Fortunately, God is willing to make allowances. His plan is not going to be derailed by the complaining that will become such a theme throughout Exodus.

We are near the beginning of the Old Testament's great story of salvation. It is already clear that if freedom comes, it will be entirely God's doing. Moses and Aaron are God's agents, but what happens does not depend on them. In the complaining Israelites we see ourselves, saved not by our own merits but by God alone.

Merciful Lord,
you know our struggle to serve you:
when sin spoils our lives
and overshadows our hearts,
come to our aid
and turn us back to you again;
through Jesus Christ our Lord.

COLLECT

Reflection by **Gillian Cooper** | 33

Exodus 6.2-13

'I will redeem you' (v.6)

Exodus is the Old Testament book that shows most clearly the hallmarks of being a compilation of traditions. The story sometimes seems disjointed, names vary, and there are differing theological emphases. We could tease apart the various strands, with the help of the scholars, but better perhaps to live with the inconsistencies and appreciate the power of the whole with its many layers of meaning. So let us treat this alternative version of the call of Moses as a clarification of the major themes of the early chapters of Exodus.

God's identity is once more at the centre. This God is Yahweh (the Lord in our English translations). His name is newly revealed, but he has been there all along, since the choice of Abraham and his family. The Lord has promised a land, and will deliver it.

Once again the Israelites do not play their part and 'know that I am the Lord your God', but it has now become irrelevant. Their cooperation is not required. Moses and Aaron are sent straight to Pharaoh to get on with the job of salvation anyway.

Here we see an emphasis on the power of the God of Exodus who is also our God. Resistance is futile, whether it comes from doubtful Israelites, a despotic Pharaoh, or the powers of sin and death. The 'outstretched arm and mighty acts of judgement' will bring redemption.

COLLECT

Merciful Lord,
absolve your people from their offences,
that through your bountiful goodness
we may all be delivered from the chains of those sins
which by our frailty we have committed;
grant this, heavenly Father,
for Jesus Christ's sake, our blessed Lord and Saviour,
who is alive and reigns with you,
in the unity of the Holy Spirit,
one God, now and for ever.

Reflection by **Gillian Cooper**

Psalm **32** *or* 120, **121**, 122
Exodus 7.8-end
Hebrews 11.1-16

Saturday 17 March

Exodus 7.8-end

'... until now you have not listened' (v.16)

So the battle begins in earnest. Who can perform the best tricks? Today it is a draw.

The story of the plagues is difficult for today's readers. It seems a very primitive way for God to operate. Why not just cut to the end and get the people out? Who needs this display of magic? Then there is the issue of the blood in the Nile, and similarly unpleasant things to come. It is the ordinary people of Egypt who suffer.

Let us try to think ourselves into the mind of the writers of Exodus. They know all the stories; everyone knows the stories – they have been told and retold down the centuries, embellished no doubt, their order confused, and there is no hope of reconstructing events as they happened. The final authors/editors attempt to make sense of it all. They describe a dramatic battle. On the one side is the tyrant, the Pharaoh, who imagines himself to have ultimate power over the land of Egypt. On the other are Moses and Aaron. What Pharaoh so far fails to realize is that Moses and Aaron are not alone. Behind them, calling the shots, is Yahweh their God. Prolonging the agony for Egypt makes the achievement of freedom all the greater. 'Look what God did for us!' we imagine the first readers exclaiming.

'Look what God did for us!' we exclaim as we look at a cross.

Merciful Lord,
you know our struggle to serve you:
when sin spoils our lives
and overshadows our hearts,
come to our aid
and turn us back to you again;
through Jesus Christ our Lord.

COLLECT

Reflection by **Gillian Cooper** | 35

Monday 19 March
Joseph of Nazareth

Psalms 25, 147.1-12
Isaiah 11.1-10
Matthew 13.54-end

Isaiah 11.1-10

'... the root of Jesse shall stand as a signal to the peoples' (v.10)

In a welcome respite from the Egyptian plagues, we miss frogs and gnats in order to celebrate St Joseph with Isaiah's beautiful vision of peace.

It is through Joseph that Matthew's Gospel traces Jesus' ancestry. Jesus is a descendant of Jesse, a new David, a king of the Jews. Throughout their history the people of Israel had a love/hate relationship with kings. When they crowned their first king, Saul, God disapproved, the Old Testament writers tell us. Kings can turn into tyrants, and will not always make wise choices. So it proved, according to the story told by the biblical historians. The ideal of kingship remained, however, despite the failings of actual kings. There was still the dream of a king who would genuinely represent God's own rule on earth. The result would be an almost unimaginable, impossible peace and prosperity.

Today reminds us that the prophecy has been fulfilled – in part. The king has come, though in a quiet and unexpected way. God's kingdom exists on earth as in heaven – almost. But wolves still kill lambs, and the meek of the earth still suffer. The establishment of the kingdom still has some way to go.

Isaiah's vision is still our vision. We know a little more now about the king's identity: Jesus, son of David, a member of the family of wise Joseph. We still dream of the day when his reign will come on earth.

COLLECT

God our Father,
who from the family of your servant David
raised up Joseph the carpenter
to be the guardian of your incarnate Son
and husband of the Blessed Virgin Mary:
give us grace to follow him
in faithful obedience to your commands;
through Jesus Christ your Son our Lord,
who is alive and reigns with you,
in the unity of the Holy Spirit,
one God, now and for ever.

36 | *Reflection by* **Gillian Cooper**

Psalms **35**, 123 *or* **132**, 133
Exodus 8.20-end
Hebrews 11.32 – 12.2

Tuesday 20 March

Exodus 8.20-end
'Pray for me' (v.28)

The battle continues, but Pharaoh is weakening. His magicians have admitted defeat, whereas there seems no limit to the horrors Moses and Aaron are prepared to inflict on the poor Egyptians. In an uncomfortable episode, Moses lies to Pharaoh about the reason the Israelites need to leave Egypt, and Pharaoh, extraordinarily, gives them permission to go, asking for their prayers. He changes his mind, however, when the plague of flies disappears before their departure, in what looks like a tactical error on the part of Moses. There is much more to come before God's people can leave. The new element here is that the Israelites are protected from the effects of the plague.

The story of the plagues has traditionally been interpreted as a classic account of a battle between good and evil. God fights the forces of darkness to win the victory of salvation for his people. For Christians, of course, this foreshadows an even greater battle and act of salvation. It may be hard to ignore the human elements of the story: Pharaoh is not entirely unsympathetic, with his desire to defend his people and his request for prayer; Moses is manipulative. In the end, though, the pattern of request and refusal, and plagues delivered and removed, heightens the readers' tension. We understand that something unbelievably bad is coming, and we know that if salvation is won, it will be associated with death.

Most merciful God,
who by the death and resurrection of your Son Jesus Christ
delivered and saved the world:
grant that by faith in him who suffered on the cross
we may triumph in the power of his victory;
through Jesus Christ your Son our Lord,
who is alive and reigns with you,
in the unity of the Holy Spirit,
one God, now and for ever.

COLLECT

Reflection by **Gillian Cooper** | 37

Wednesday 21 March

Psalms **55**, 124 *or* **119.153-end**
Exodus 9.1-12
Hebrews 12.3-13

Exodus 9.1-12

'But the Lord hardened the heart of Pharaoh' (v.12)

Things are getting serious now. The previous disasters have been bad enough, but now livestock are dying and people are being seriously disabled by boils. The plagues have become life-threatening. Tension is increasing. Surely Pharaoh has to crack soon? But Pharaoh is in essence a tyrant like any other, despite his occasional concessions, and we know from our experience of Pharaoh's contemporary equivalents that it is almost impossible for a tyrant to back down once a stance has been taken.

Life in the Nile delta was precarious in ancient times, and any of the plagues could have happened in the natural course of events. We are not, however, intended to read this story as a history of natural disasters. In some places it has an almost pantomime quality: Yes he will! No he won't! My magic is better than yours! The good hero is destined to win in the end, no matter how powerful the evil king. We can imagine the fun involved in the retelling of the story to children down the years.

Yet the story is, of course, deadly serious. The repetition of the pattern of Pharaoh's agreement and refusal, of the plague imposed and lifted, in the end causes us horror rather than amusement, as we contemplate what may happen next. This is a story about salvation, and we are being told over and over what an extraordinary and difficult matter that is.

COLLECT

Most merciful God,
who by the death and resurrection of your Son Jesus Christ
delivered and saved the world:
grant that by faith in him who suffered on the cross
we may triumph in the power of his victory;
through Jesus Christ your Son our Lord,
who is alive and reigns with you,
in the unity of the Holy Spirit,
one God, now and for ever.

Reflection by **Gillian Cooper**

Psalms **40**, 125 *or* **143**, 146
Exodus 9.13-end
Hebrews 12.14-end

Thursday 22 March

Exodus 9.13-end

*'... to show you my power, and to make my name resound
through all the earth' (v.16)*

So now we know. This is not about punishing the Egyptians. It is not even about freeing the Israelites. It is about God and the world.

The final editors of Exodus knew that their work would be read by the descendants of people who had experienced defeat by a succession of tyrannical emperors, and who had suffered exile from their homeland. They had good reason to doubt their God and his promises. They had lost their land and their kings, and ended up a small corner of a province of an empire, insignificant as far as the world was concerned. What would they think? That God was not very powerful? Or perhaps that God was just not very interested in them?

Remember your history, our writers tell them. Your God defeated Pharaoh and all his magicians with a prolonged demonstration of power. God kept his promises once and will do so again. Resistance to God's plan, however fierce, can only ever be temporary. It took a long time to be freed from Egypt, and even longer to make it to their promised land, but God's promises can only ever be deferred, never cancelled.

We are not yet at the end of the story. Pharaoh is still resisting. But readers then and now are invited to trust that there can only be one winner of this battle, however high the cost proves to be.

Gracious Father,
you gave up your Son
out of love for the world:
lead us to ponder the mysteries of his passion,
that we may know eternal peace
through the shedding of our Saviour's blood,
Jesus Christ our Lord.

COLLECT

Friday 23 March

Psalms **22**, 126 *or* 142, **144**
Exodus 10
Hebrews 13.1-16

Exodus 10

'... that you may tell your children and grandchildren how I have made fools of the Egyptians' (v.2)

It is a story worth telling, and the reason we have this story to read now is that it was indeed told.

The Old Testament writers place great emphasis on retelling and remembering. They know that a nation that forgets its history loses its place in the world. They know too that a nation that forgets how much it owes to its God is heading for disaster. So our author reminds us that the story of the plagues is the nation's story for all time. For many centuries to come, families will re-enact the Passover meal that heralded the Israelites' final departure from Egypt. They will remember that their escape was not easy. They will tell a story of powerful enemies, of danger, and of wavering faith in an uncertain future. But the story they tell will mostly be about the wonder of their God. They have a God who faces up to the fiercest opposition with calm planning; a God who keeps his promises no matter what; a God who cannot be beaten; a God who saves them even when they do not want to be saved; and a God who expects much from them in return.

For now, Pharaoh is weakening, but Moses is expanding his demands. The Israelites must leave all together, with all their belongings. No one is any longer pretending they will come back. Darkness descends on Egypt. We are nearing the end-game.

COLLECT

Most merciful God,
who by the death and resurrection of your Son Jesus Christ
delivered and saved the world:
grant that by faith in him who suffered on the cross
we may triumph in the power of his victory;
through Jesus Christ your Son our Lord,
who is alive and reigns with you,
in the unity of the Holy Spirit,
one God, now and for ever.

Reflection by **Gillian Cooper**

Psalms **23**, 127 *or* **147**   **Saturday 24 March**
Exodus 11
Hebrews 13.17-end

Exodus 11

'Then there will be a loud cry throughout the whole land' (v.6)

This is it, the final act. The Israelites start to get ready. The Egyptians will be glad to see the back of them, so glad that they give them all their disposable wealth to get rid of them. They do not yet know what final horror awaits them.

How high the cost of the Israelites' freedom! How high for his people the cost of Pharaoh's stubbornness! Even as we rejoice with the Israelites, we weep with the Egyptians, to whom the other plagues will soon seem as nothing in the face of their overwhelming grief.

This is a hard story to read. It seriously challenges our moral sensibilities. It has done so from the beginning, as the people of Egypt have suffered, but the slightly pantomime quality of the magic contest has mitigated our distaste. Now, however, there is no escape. Egyptian men, women and children will die, and mourn, so that God's own people can live freely. Any justifications we may create fail before that grief. In the battle between good and evil, these are innocent casualties, collateral damage. The story is what it is. We have to deal with it. We cannot pretend it is all right. Its retelling must surely be full of grief as well as rejoicing.

As we approach Holy Week, death is on our minds. Another first-born will soon die. This time, however, the cost is borne by God himself.

Gracious Father,
you gave up your Son
out of love for the world:
lead us to ponder the mysteries of his passion,
that we may know eternal peace
through the shedding of our Saviour's blood,
Jesus Christ our Lord.

COLLECT

Reflection by **Gillian Cooper**   41

Monday 26 March

Monday of Holy Week

Psalm 41
Lamentations 1.1-12*a*
Luke 22.1-23

Lamentations 1.1-12*a*

'The roads to Zion mourn ... all her gates are desolate' (v.4)

I confess that I have a penchant for films that feature dystopias. I think of *Logan's Run*, a wonderful science fiction classic from 1976 starring Jenny Agutter and Michael York. Set a long time in the future, this unlikely couple escape the clutches of their pursuers, only to find that the sanctuary they reach is a 'wasted place' – a city in ruins. Its former glory is there to glimpse – but the city is now an uninhabited wasteland. This is an Aleppo, Palmyra, Benghazi and Tripoli.

The Holy Week readings serve up plenty of paradoxes, and the evocative image of a desolate city is no exception. It prefigures the death and desertion of Good Friday. It is also a metaphor for inner grief, the death and destruction inside our souls. We mourn for the state we are in.

In this lamentation, the writer speaks for his people, but also echoes something of what Jesus' experience of Holy Week and Good Friday must be – abandoned, scorned, an object of vilification and wrath. What has he done to deserve this? 'My God, my God, why have you forsaken me?' (Matthew 27.46).

Yet Holy Week is also about remembering that no matter how deserted we may feel, God never abandons us. We are ultimately raised up from despair and death. That is the paradox of Good Friday. Jesus becomes the desolate one on our behalf, so that we might never be without God again. Jesus becomes forsaken so we might forever have eternity with God.

COLLECT

Almighty and everlasting God,
who in your tender love towards the human race
    sent your Son our Saviour Jesus Christ
to take upon him our flesh
and to suffer death upon the cross:
grant that we may follow the example of his patience and humility,
and also be made partakers of his resurrection;
through Jesus Christ your Son our Lord,
who is alive and reigns with you,
in the unity of the Holy Spirit,
one God, now and for ever.

Psalm 27
Lamentations 3.1-18
Luke 22.[24-38] 39-53

Tuesday 27 March
Tuesday of Holy Week

Lamentations 3.1-18

*'... he has besieged and enveloped me with bitterness
and tribulation' (v.5)*

The writer of Lamentations offers us a meditation of deep despair –
a diminishment of his humanity that is disturbing and disabling, and a
sense that God, no less, is 'afflicting' Jeremiah. But all of it is felt inside
the body of the writer – and keenly so. Jeremiah laments that God will
slowly humiliate and obliterate him. He internalizes this, as a process
of corrosion, wasting and disablement.

Jeremiah's lament is about as dark and depressing as it can get. So
what are we to say of God in all this? Three things, it seems to me.

First, that God will never leave us or forsake us. God does not know
how to be absent in our lives or our world. So even when we think we
experience God's absence, God is there. Second, and to paraphrase
C. S. Lewis, God whispers in our pleasure, but shouts in our pain. God
will yet find a way to shine a light in this darkness of ours. Third, that
'all shall be well', as Julian of Norwich so poignantly expressed it. We
are held by God, and will be held and raised up.

In Holy Week it is Jesus who, in taking on our humanity, must also take
on the darkest hours of isolation and desolation. In his life, they are
fully assumed so we can be fully redeemed. God knows what we feel;
in Jesus, it is known and taken to the heart of the creator, where it is
held, treasured and transformed.

> True and humble king,
> hailed by the crowd as Messiah:
> grant us the faith to know you and love you,
> that we may be found beside you
> on the way of the cross,
> which is the path of glory.

COLLECT

Reflection by **Martyn Percy**   43

Wednesday 28 March
Wednesday of Holy Week

Psalm 102 [*or* 102.1-18]
Wisdom 1.16 – 2.1; 2.12-22
or Jeremiah 11.18-20
Luke 22.54-end

Jeremiah 11.18-20

'... a gentle lamb led to the slaughter' (v.19)

From the first Easter, Christians have proclaimed that 'the Lamb that was slain' takes away the sins of the world. Here at Christ Church in Oxford, the college has a painting from the 1580s by Annibale Carracci known as *The Butcher's Shop*. It portrays a passive lamb about to be slaughtered, surrounded by other butchered meat ready for sale. The lamb in the picture looks resigned; it knows what is coming next.

A paradox of Christian faith is proclaiming Jesus as both the Great Shepherd of the Sheep and the Lamb of God. As any Sunday school child will testify, images of Jesus carrying a young lamb aloft on his shoulder are powerful and resonant. Jesus rescues the lost; he raises up and restores the lost sheep that would otherwise have perished.

But Holy Week also does something unusual to this Great Shepherd of the Sheep. It turns Jesus into just another one of the flock, and leads him to be butchered at the cross in the same way as countless thousands of others would die that year, at the hands of fickle Roman justice. Led like a lamb to the slaughter.

Yet a faith that takes its shepherd and turns him into a sheep tells a deeper story. Christian tradition portrays Jesus as the Saviour, and in so doing reaches back to the Jewish perception of the Passover, of scape-goating and of the Pascal lamb. Here, in this death, and by the shedding of this blood, God will redeem his people. To be the victor, you must first be the victim.

COLLECT

Almighty and everlasting God,
who in your tender love towards the human race
    sent your Son our Saviour Jesus Christ
to take upon him our flesh
and to suffer death upon the cross:
grant that we may follow the example of his patience and humility,
and also be made partakers of his resurrection;
through Jesus Christ your Son our Lord,
who is alive and reigns with you,
in the unity of the Holy Spirit,
one God, now and for ever.

Reflection by **Martyn Percy**

Psalms 42, 43
Leviticus 16.2-24
Luke 23.1-25

Thursday 29 March
Maundy Thursday

Leviticus 16.2-24
'Thus he shall make atonement ...' (v.16)

At the centre of Good Friday and Maundy Thursday is the image of the slaughtered lamb who atones for our lives. This animal offering to procure our righteousness before God – scripted by the Old Testament, and then reframed in the New Testament – is what links the faith of Christianity to its parental Judaism. And today, the image offers three ways of looking at the coming sacrifice.

First, this slaughtered lamb reflects a kind of tame compliance. In silence, Jesus absorbs the pain and the hatred that is visited upon him. The centre of Good Friday comes in the realization that this hurt and violence will not be passed on – they are to be absorbed by God.

Second, the blood and the wounds are salvific. Jesus' blood is somehow nourishing, and to feed off it is to participate in the abundant life of God. To be covered by the blood of the lamb symbolizes not only purity, but a new kind of intensity, in which the life of God washes away the pain, sickness and violence of the world.

Third, we know that Jesus' last words from the cross will be concerned not with protestations of his innocence, but with the spreading of forgiveness. Jesus seems to be powerfully aware that his executioners really *don't* know what they are doing. They too are simple instruments in a system where this engineering of cruel death is part of everyday life. With Jesus' words, our sins of ignorance are absolved.

And so the Lamb of God who was slain for the world invites us to his supper.

True and humble king,
hailed by the crowd as Messiah:
grant us the faith to know you and love you,
that we may be found beside you
on the way of the cross,
which is the path of glory.

COLLECT

Friday 30 March
Good Friday

Psalm 69
Genesis 22.1-18
John 19.38-end
or Hebrews 10.1-10

Genesis 22.1-18
'God himself will provide the lamb' (v.8)

It is easy to forget how precious Isaac was to his father and mother. Earlier in Genesis, 'the Lord appeared to Abraham' in the form of three mysterious men (Genesis 18.1). Abraham receives the strangers and gives them hospitality. These men then announce that Abraham's wife, the barren Sarah, now in her nineties (Genesis 17.17), will soon give birth to a son. Sarah laughs at this, but the three visitors reply gnomically: 'Is anything too hard for the Lord?' Nine months later, Sarah gives birth to Isaac.

So, what is too hard for the Lord? The answer is nothing, of course. But today of all days takes us to a place that is very hard, one that no human would ever want to arrive at. For who can ever sacrifice their own child?

No parent can imagine what Abraham is doing. But this story is not about appeasing the gods of old with a precious blood sacrifice, let alone killing the innocent to satisfy the God of Abraham, Isaac, Jacob and Moses. This story is about something else; it is a story that ends self-sacrifice.

There is nothing precious that we own or love that we can sacrifice in order to close the gap between ourselves and God. God, in Christ, has already reached us. The cross of Christ is God's signature and a pledge: we are fully loved. Nothing we can do, say or offer can change that. Even if we disown him, he will not disown us. That's why the sacrifice is God's, not ours. Truly, today is Good Friday. — *SILENCE*

COLLECT

· So we pray

Almighty Father,
look with mercy on this your family
for which our Lord Jesus Christ was content to be betrayed
      and given up into the hands of sinners
      and to suffer death upon the cross;
who is alive and glorified with you and the Holy Spirit,
one God, now and for ever.

— *silence.*

| *Reflection by* **Martyn Percy**

Psalm 142
Hosea 6.1-6
John 2.18-22

Saturday 31 March
Easter Eve

Hosea 6.1-6

'... the knowledge of God rather than burnt-offerings' (v.6)

Lent is over – yet on Easter Eve comes the call: time to repent! Talk of repentance makes modern-day Christians nervous, even squeamish. We are embarrassed by the stereotype of old-fashioned preachers hammering on about sin and guilt. We rush to assert that Jesus isn't really like that. He came out of love; he wants to help us. He knows us deep inside and feels our every pain, and his healing love sets us free.

That's true, of course, but nevertheless, repentance is the doorway to the spiritual life, the only way to begin. It is also the path itself, the only way to continue. Anything else is foolishness and self-delusion.

The ancient Christian literature on repentance can be quite beautiful – full of simplicity, humility, and peace. Those who know themselves to be so greatly forgiven are far from gloomy, but are flooded with joy and deep tranquillity. Those who are forgiven much, love much. They find it hard to hold grudges against others; they find it hard to hold anything in this life too tightly. For Christians, two things are ever-linked: sorrow over sin, and gratitude for forgiveness.

The resurrection will burst this all asunder. We are now asked to greet our saviour. Our sacrifices of old are to be replaced with a new knowledge of God. As we wait in darkness, the light is about the dawn: repentance will be met with forgiveness; mourning with joy; death with life. And so we turn to the One who is life, light and joy – who in his death and sacrifice, has freed us from death.

Grant, Lord,
that we who are baptized into the death
of your Son our Saviour Jesus Christ
may continually put to death our evil desires
and be buried with him;
and that through the grave and gate of death
we may pass to our joyful resurrection;
through his merits,
who died and was buried and rose again for us,
your Son Jesus Christ our Lord.

COLLECT

Morning Prayer – a simple form

Preparation

O Lord, open our lips
and our mouth shall proclaim your praise.

A prayer of thanksgiving for Lent *(for Passiontide see p. 50)*

Blessed are you, Lord God of our salvation,
to you be glory and praise for ever.
In the darkness of our sin you have shone in our hearts
to give the light of the knowledge of the glory of God
in the face of Jesus Christ.
Open our eyes to acknowledge your presence,
that freed from the misery of sin and shame
we may grow into your likeness from glory to glory.
Blessed be God, Father, Son and Holy Spirit.
Blessed be God for ever.

Word of God

Psalmody *(the psalm or psalms listed for the day)*

**Glory to the Father and to the Son
and to the Holy Spirit;
as it was in the beginning is now:
and shall be for ever. Amen.**

Reading from Holy Scripture *(one or both of the passages set for the day)*

Reflection

The Benedictus (The Song of Zechariah) *(see opposite page)*

Prayers

Intercessions – a time of prayer for the day and its tasks, the world and its need, the church and her life.

The Collect for the Day

The Lord's Prayer *(see p. 51)*

Conclusion

A blessing or the Grace *(see p. 51)*, or a concluding response

Let us bless the Lord
Thanks be to God

Benedictus (The Song of Zechariah)

1 Blessed be the Lord the God of Israel, ◆
   who has come to his people and set them free.

2 He has raised up for us a mighty Saviour, ◆
   born of the house of his servant David.

3 Through his holy prophets God promised of old ◆
   to save us from our enemies,
       from the hands of all that hate us,

4 To show mercy to our ancestors, ◆
   and to remember his holy covenant.

5 This was the oath God swore to our father Abraham: ◆
   to set us free from the hands of our enemies,

6 Free to worship him without fear, ◆
   holy and righteous in his sight
       all the days of our life.

7 And you, child, shall be called the prophet of the Most High, ◆
   for you will go before the Lord to prepare his way,

8 To give his people knowledge of salvation ◆
   by the forgiveness of all their sins.

9 In the tender compassion of our God ◆
   the dawn from on high shall break upon us,

10 To shine on those who dwell in darkness
       and the shadow of death, ◆
   and to guide our feet into the way of peace.

Luke 1.68-79

**Glory to the Father and to the Son
and to the Holy Spirit;
as it was in the beginning is now:
and shall be for ever. Amen.**

Seasonal Prayers of Thanksgiving

Passiontide

Blessed are you, Lord God of our salvation,
to you be praise and glory for ever.
As a man of sorrows and acquainted with grief
your only Son was lifted up
that he might draw the whole world to himself.
May we walk this day in the way of the cross
and always be ready to share its weight,
declaring your love for all the world.
Blessed be God, Father, Son and Holy Spirit.
Blessed be God for ever.

At Any Time

Blessed are you, creator of all,
to you be praise and glory for ever.
As your dawn renews the face of the earth
bringing light and life to all creation,
may we rejoice in this day you have made;
as we wake refreshed from the depths of sleep,
open our eyes to behold your presence
and strengthen our hands to do your will,
that the world may rejoice and give you praise.
Blessed be God, Father, Son and Holy Spirit.
Blessed be God for ever.

after Lancelot Andrewes (1626)

The Lord's Prayer and The Grace

Our Father in heaven,
hallowed be your name,
your kingdom come,
your will be done,
on earth as in heaven.
Give us today our daily bread.
Forgive us our sins
as we forgive those who sin against us.
Lead us not into temptation
but deliver us from evil.
For the kingdom, the power,
and the glory are yours
now and for ever.
Amen.

(or)

Our Father, who art in heaven,
hallowed be thy name;
thy kingdom come;
thy will be done;
on earth as it is in heaven.
Give us this day our daily bread.
And forgive us our trespasses,
as we forgive those who trespass against us.
And lead us not into temptation;
but deliver us from evil.
For thine is the kingdom,
the power and the glory,
for ever and ever.
Amen.

The grace of our Lord Jesus Christ,
and the love of God,
and the fellowship of the Holy Spirit,
be with us all evermore.
Amen.

An Order for Night Prayer (Compline)

Preparation

The Lord almighty grant us a quiet night and a perfect end.
Amen.

Our help is in the name of the Lord
who made heaven and earth.

A period of silence for reflection on the past day may follow.

The following or other suitable words of penitence may be used

**Most merciful God,
we confess to you,
before the whole company of heaven and one another,
that we have sinned in thought, word and deed
and in what we have failed to do.
Forgive us our sins,
heal us by your Spirit
and raise us to new life in Christ. Amen.**

O God, make speed to save us.
O Lord, make haste to help us.

**Glory to the Father and to the Son
and to the Holy Spirit;
as it was in the beginning is now
and shall be for ever. Amen.
Alleluia.**

The following or another suitable hymn may be sung

Before the ending of the day,
Creator of the world, we pray
That you, with steadfast love, would keep
Your watch around us while we sleep.

From evil dreams defend our sight,
From fears and terrors of the night;
Tread underfoot our deadly foe
That we no sinful thought may know.

O Father, that we ask be done
Through Jesus Christ, your only Son;
And Holy Spirit, by whose breath
Our souls are raised to life from death.

The Word of God

Psalmody

One or more of Psalms 4, 91 or 134 may be used.

Psalm 134

1   Come, bless the Lord, all you servants of the Lord, ♦
      you that by night stand in the house of the Lord.

2   Lift up your hands towards the sanctuary ♦
      and bless the Lord.

3   The Lord who made heaven and earth ♦
      give you blessing out of Zion.

**Glory to the Father and to the Son
and to the Holy Spirit;
as it was in the beginning is now
and shall be for ever. Amen.**

Scripture Reading

*One of the following short lessons or another suitable
passage is read*

You, O Lord, are in the midst of us and we are called by your
name; leave us not, O Lord our God.

Jeremiah 14.9

(or)

Be sober, be vigilant, because your adversary the devil is
prowling round like a roaring lion, seeking for someone
to devour. Resist him, strong in the faith.

1 Peter 5.8,9

(or)

The servants of the Lamb shall see the face of God, whose name
will be on their foreheads. There will be no more night: they will
not need the light of a lamp or the light of the sun, for God will
be their light, and they will reign for ever and ever.

Revelation 22.4,5

Into your hands, O Lord, I commend my spirit.
Into your hands, O Lord, I commend my spirit.
For you have redeemed me, Lord God of truth.
I commend my spirit.
Glory to the Father and to the Son
and to the Holy Spirit.
Into your hands, O Lord, I commend my spirit.

Or, in Easter

Into your hands, O Lord, I commend my spirit.
　Alleluia, alleluia.
Into your hands, O Lord, I commend my spirit.
　Alleluia, alleluia.
For you have redeemed me, Lord God of truth.
Alleluia, alleluia.
Glory to the Father and to the Son
and to the Holy Spirit.
Into your hands, O Lord, I commend my spirit.
　Alleluia, alleluia.

Keep me as the apple of your eye.
Hide me under the shadow of your wings.

Gospel Canticle

Nunc Dimittis (The Song of Simeon)

Save us, O Lord, while waking,
and guard us while sleeping,
that awake we may watch with Christ
and asleep may rest in peace.

1　Now, Lord, you let your servant go in peace:
　your word has been fulfilled.

2　My own eyes have seen the salvation
　which you have prepared in the sight of every people;

3　A light to reveal you to the nations
　and the glory of your people Israel.

Luke 2.29-32

Glory to the Father and to the Son
and to the Holy Spirit;
as it was in the beginning is now
and shall be for ever. Amen.

Save us, O Lord, while waking,
and guard us while sleeping,
that awake we may watch with Christ
and asleep may rest in peace.

Prayers

Intercessions and thanksgivings may be offered here.

The Collect

Visit this place, O Lord, we pray,
and drive far from it the snares of the enemy;
may your holy angels dwell with us and guard us in peace,
and may your blessing be always upon us;
through Jesus Christ our Lord.
Amen.

The Lord's Prayer (see p. 51) may be said.

The Conclusion

In peace we will lie down and sleep;
for you alone, Lord, make us dwell in safety.

Abide with us, Lord Jesus,
for the night is at hand and the day is now past.

As the night watch looks for the morning,
so do we look for you, O Christ.

[Come with the dawning of the day
and make yourself known in the breaking of the bread.]

The Lord bless us and watch over us;
the Lord make his face shine upon us and be gracious to us;
the Lord look kindly on us and give us peace.
Amen.

Love what you've read?

Why not consider using
Reflections for Daily Prayer
all year round? We also
publish these meditations
on Bible readings in an
annual format, containing
material for the entire
Church year.

The volume for 2018/19
will be published in May
2018 and features
contributions from a host
of distinguished writers:
Justine Allain Chapman,
Kate Bruce, Steven Croft,
Paula Gooder, Peter Graystone, Helen-Ann Hartley,
David Hoyle, Graham James, Jan McFarlane,
Libby Lane, Gordon Mursell, Helen Orchard,
John Perumbalath, David Runcorn, Sarah Rowland
Jones, Harry Steele, Richard Sudworth, Angela Tilby,
Graham Tomlin and Margaret Whipp.

Reflections for Daily Prayer:
Advent 2018 to the eve of Advent 2019

ISBN 978 1 78140 007 4
£16.99 • Available May 2018

Can't wait for next year?

You can still pick up this year's edition of *Reflections*,
direct from us (at **www.chpublishing.co.uk**) or from
your local Christian bookshop.

Reflections for Daily Prayer:
Advent 2017 to the eve of Advent 2018

ISBN 978 1 78140 019 7
£16.99 • Available Now

REFLECTIONS FOR DAILY PRAYER
App

Make Bible study and reflection a part of your routine wherever you go with the Reflections for Daily Prayer App for Apple and Android devices.

Download the app for free from the App Store (Apple devices) or Google Play (Android devices) and receive a week's worth of reflections free. Then purchase a monthly, three-monthly or annual subscription to receive up-to-date content.

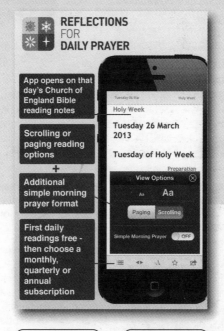

App opens on that day's Church of England Bible reading notes

Scrolling or paging reading options

Additional simple morning prayer format

First daily readings free – then choose a monthly, quarterly or annual subscription

REFLECTIONS FOR SUNDAYS

Reflections for Sundays offers over 250 reflections on the Principal Readings for every Sunday and major Holy Day in Year B, from the same experienced team of writers that have made *Reflections for Daily Prayer* so successful. For each Sunday and major Holy Day, they provide:

- full lectionary details for the Principal Service
- a reflection on each Old Testament reading (both Continuous and Related)
- a reflection on the Epistle
- a reflection on the Gospel.

This book also contains a substantial introduction to the Gospels of Mark and Luke, written by Paula Gooder.

£14.99 • 288 pages
ISBN 978 1 78140 030 2

Also available in Kindle and epub formats

REFLECTIONS ON THE PSALMS

£14.99 • 192 pages
ISBN 978 0 7151 4490 9

Reflections on the Psalms provides original and insightful meditations on each of the Bible's 150 Psalms.

Each reflection is accompanied by its corresponding Psalm refrain and prayer from the *Common Worship Psalter*, making this a valuable resource for personal or devotional use.

Specially written introductions by Paula Gooder and Steven Croft explore the Psalms and the Bible and the Psalms in the life of the Church.